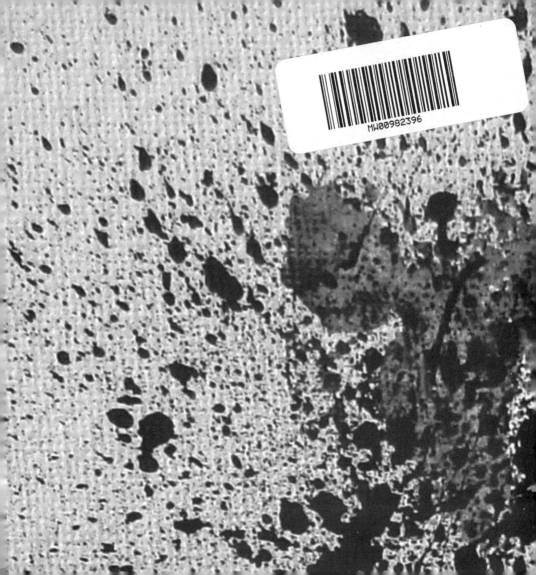

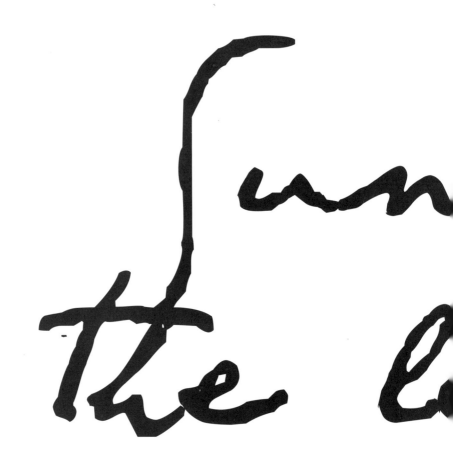

A POEM

JIM JOHNSTONE
JULIENNE LOTTERING

play,

counts

Tightrope Books

for the love
of poetry

Tightrope Books
602 Markham Street, Toronto, Ontario, Canada M6G 2L8
www.tightropebooks.com

Editor: Ray Hsu   Copyeditor: Shirarose Wilensky   Book Design: Karen Correia Da Silva

Produced with the assistance of the Canada Council for the Arts and the Ontario Arts Council.

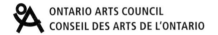

PRINTED IN CANADA.

Library and Archives Canada Cataloguing in Publication

Johnstone, Jim, 1978-
Sunday, the locusts / Jim Johnstone and Julienne Lottering.

A poem.
ISBN 978-1-926639-36-9

I. Lottering, Julienne II. Title.

PS8619.O489S86 2011   C811'.6   C2011-900255-8

for the University of Toronto

. . . These locusts were once men, before the birth of the Muses, and when the Muses were born and song appeared, some of the men were so overcome with delight that they sang and sang, forgetting food and drink, until at last unconsciously they died.

Plato – *Phaedrus*

The pursuit of knowledge feeds us. Buildings, classrooms, laboratories, cafeterias. This has been much of our landscape, flickering in our field of vision. All these places are built on ideas of development, stages, hierarchy.

There was once a pecking order that some folks called *The Great Chain of Being*. It was convenient to know who was subject to whom. Someone dissected, something was dissected, down past the genes. The architecture out in the city is the lattice of our bodies.

But somewhere in the thing dissected was the feeling of a landscape brushing by, the evening roaring. Perhaps alone now, but for a brief life lived in a chorus that sought a path through the atmosphere. What language is this feeling? Why is it so familiar to our mouths? What creation myth have we forgotten?

Ray Hsu, October 2010

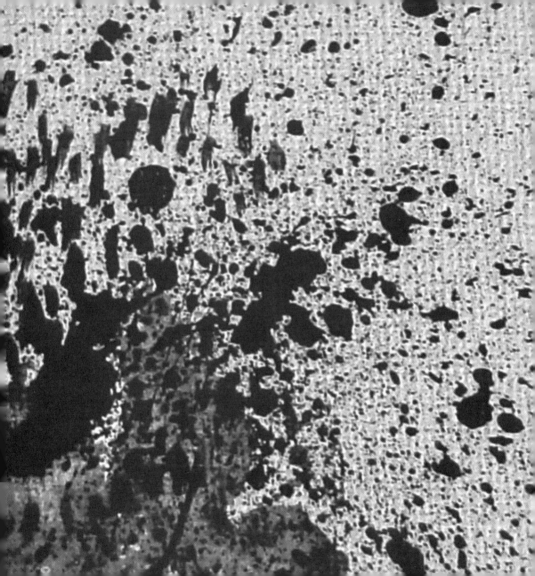

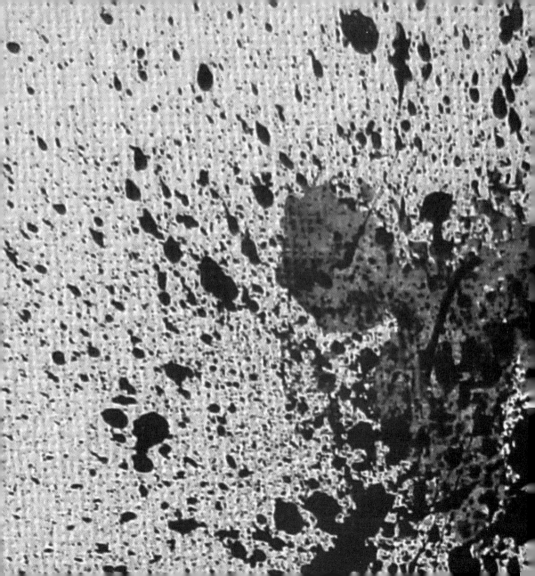

each instant, a new spindle

skull / heart / pelvis / fibula

if not here

then nowhere

antennae / ostia / thorax / tarsus

carbon alight, limits reached

(North Atlantic: 50°50′N, 25°15′W)

U211's firing squad, the ocean's cork-like breach.
It will be an hour before our stanchion is flayed in
escort – survivors eclipsed, scattered to the deep.

Each mouth dissolves like the heart of a pearl.
Remerciez. Remerciez, Madame Forget. At her name
I leap toward star shells, swim bladder a drained
thermos at my side. Split, the Atlantic continues
crafting waves – cells mushrooming, revisiting
their beginnings.

I wake in the ash and the wind
of the night, breathless.

                        Forsaken by a flood
                        of ships
     I scull forward –

          gills unsettled, body a knot
          in the current's

   labyrinth of applause.

Later, bent beneath the harbour's
weight,

                        my skin is a runway
                        for touch –
    the city's fingers,

         their font of shell
         and sand.

Touch travels forward, winged, swallows rail and rock. Sunday, the locusts that pass overhead are human, hum with electricity – stars shingled to shore. A glittering cloud, they lay their hands between narrow worlds, bloody their own doors to endure.

Kingdom *Animalia*

Phylum *Arthropoda*

Class *Insecta*

Order *Orthoptera*

Suborder *Caelifera*

Family *Acrididae*

Subfamily *Cyrtacanthacridinae*

Genus *Schistocerca*

Slowly, I drift from the articulation
of the sea —

       the tide's glottal
       stop.

Locusts rise, spread their wings
over waves like scrolls,

ghost Toronto's
orthography with flight.

In the city's hub my throat
constricts —

       an avaricious stone,
       unmoved.

See thru

>to the surf

>its face diamond,
>mouth

>contracted.

In any old hotel room, an old upright stands – the
music of a frail metal bridge looking out over the
bluffs. Automotive pumps, manuals, hoses / wait
for the

>garage to empty.

Insect Biology and Recognition

Egg: the ovipositor a froth that hardens. eggs covered / rice shaped. 7-8 mm long.

Nymph: worm through the soil. *surface*. two phases in colour / behaviour.

Adult: pink may become rose or orange brown. e.g. in solitarious forms. mature forewings are peg-like, several generations per year.

Warehouses flood streams
     where trout
     once surfaced,

          flashing silver against
     orange leaves.

Raccoons slither into trees of our own
light's making.

I slog through alluvium –
sediment narrows
against my slender legs.

     I know the sea the way
     I know the hull of my own
     skin.

Instar (6)

A mad sum, white dwarfs. Names extinguished in moonlight. Forward, dogs nose direction, freshly tilled earth at their nostrils, burial markers lost.

Simeon, Judah, Joseph, Benjamin, Dan, Asher, Aaron, Caleb, Joshua, Israel.

The field's brocade

fixed before silt

        was borne away.

Stratum

glass

lean to

swamp

river silt

dolostone

beach sand

conglomerate

S. Gregaria

limestone

vanadium

lamina

femur

chalk

(32°44´00˝N, 16°58´00˝W)

Plastic flamingos in the library,
hollow foxgloves.

Deposed of mirth, mannered,
my path knots

       like script,

opens with the patience
of handwriting.

I search for the miraculous
in everything –

       air chucks,
       watchmaker lathes,

the ground not worth
digging.

Locust and drosophila *pale* gene homology

```
lmi   CGCAAUAGGAGGCAAAAAUG GGACCA AG
dme   A--CCGCAACUA--------UUAUU GGACCA AA
dsi   A--CCGCAACUA--------UUAUU GGACCA AA
dse   A--CCGCAACUA--------UUAUU GGACCA AA
der   A--CCGCAACUA--------UUAUU GGACCA AA
dya   A--CCGCAACUA--------UUAUU GGACCA AA
dan   A--CCGCAACUA--------UUAUU GGACCA AA
dpe   A--CCGCAACUA--------UUAUU GGACCA AA
dps   A--CCGCAACUA--------UUAUU GGACCA AA
dwi   -------------AACUA--------UUAUU GGACCA AA
dvi   AACCCCAACUAAAUAUUAUU GGACCA AA
dgr   AUCCCCCACUAAAUAAUAUU GGACCA AA
dmo   A--UCCCAACUAAAUAUUAUU GGACCA AA
```

I offer my voice to the moon, return to land after years at sea and still the locusts sing. Portative organs. Wings purled, beating en masse.

Lysias, in absence, talks the currents to their stations. Sails awry on square-rigged masts. In the arms of the city my pulse kicks silt like a windmill – I forget to eat and drink until I die.

On the horizon,
silhouettes –

      Lotus Eaters who care
      not for home.

Their voices mute
the highway –

            its singing
    pins
        of rain,

    detonating clay.

וררוי

A rough glimmer – blackflies root in my skin, rush towards singular deaths. Wings, fingertips, the annexation of leverage. Flight an effortless distraction – no way to slake hunger with a killdeer's eggs, their gleam of polished stone. Taking one in my fist I bear the relentless sigh of yolk, the flap and stir of home – a simple map. The wind will pick up if I'm going to live much longer, moving from bird to bird, sky to sky.

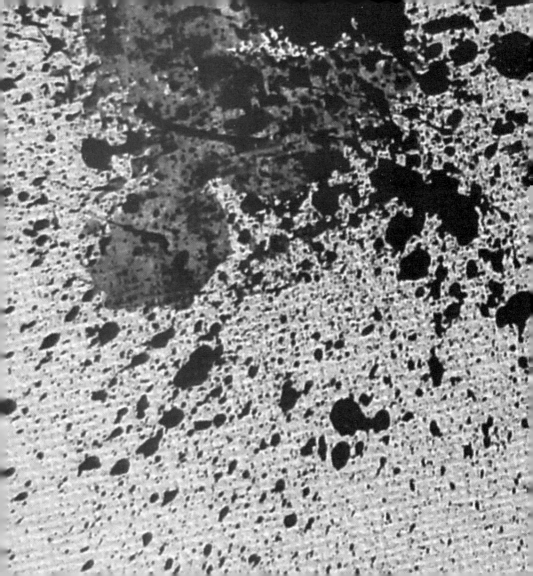

Instar (c)

Clothed in lightning, an opera
of fat sparks,

you're the first blooded
creature
                    I touch.

                Albumin, urea, silk.

    Hemocytes

            leaving
and returning
                    changed.

(33°-29° N 34°-36° E)

A green and black mass, locusts river the lowlands, engulf leaves of glass. Flare and rattle.

Swathed in passage, you lower your skirt to landfill, collect kilogram after kilogram of debris. Inkblots choke the horizon. We sleep knowing these swarms have become the kingdom and the power and glory forever and ever. *Amen.*

here's the folly of home / sandpipers / blackbirds drifting to the St. Lawrence

here's a scimitar / its blade a fluent point

here, invertebrates divide / lineal migrants moored at the river's spine

here's an eye / a sky clearing moon

The viaduct's lattice mimics
the architecture
of your spine –

                    vermiculate links

            smeared with a rosary
            of sweat.

Together, we trace cairns
where buffalos

                    were run from cliffs,

our fingers anticline,
our bodies
vans beating the air.

All night I imagine you dreaming in a strange bed, recumbent, your left hand broken by the moon. An amalgam of scrap-iron and melted sky, even insects won't sleep here – shells reverberating, flooding the atmosphere.

You tell me you remember open air, cattle and their huge eyes. Brushing sand from my skin, your handprints flush with warmth, burgeon underground.

Origin of Species, Redacted

Locusts ~~are sometimes blown to great distances from the land; I myself caught one 370 miles from the coast of Africa, and have heard of others caught at greater distances. The Rev. R. T. Lowe informed Sir. C. Lyell that in November, 1844, swarms of locusts visited the island of Madeira. They were in countless numbers,~~ as thick as the flakes of snow ~~in the heaviest snowstorm, and extended upwards as far as could be seen with a telescope. During two or three days they slowly careered round and round in an immense ellipse, at least five or six miles in diameter, and at night~~ alight~~ed on the taller trees, which were completely coated with them. They~~ then disappear~~ed over the sea, as suddenly as they had appeared, and have not since visited the island. Now, in parts of Natal it is believed by some farmers, though on insufficient evidence, the~~ injurious seeds ~~are introduced into their grass-land in the dung~~ left by ~~the~~ great flights ~~of locusts which often visit the country. In consequence of this belief Mr. Weale sent me in a letter a small packet of the dried pellets, out of which I extracted under the microscope several seeds, and raised from them seven grass plants, belonging to two species, of two genera. Hence a swarm of locusts, such as that which visited Madeira, might readily be the means of introducing several kinds of plants into an island lying far~~ from the mainland.

Freedom is nothing else but a chance to be better. What flag, what ravelled seam binds us like claws bordering a ring?

A procession of rags is fastened together and freed to sing. *Remerciez. Remerciez, Madame Forget.* Frontal lobe gone sour, gone dark with a windowpane's rifled shards, the city we helped build has crumbled. A gravedigger mines its trifling mouth –

a windmill of dendrites

mandible / trachea / clavicle

the prisoners knot

Attica! Attica!

labrum / clypeus / gena

routed clockwise over bone

Mercuric, centipedes press in,
their mouths
a familiar language.

        Heard in reverse, speech
        is untenable, shifts
  like
           a hurried arc
        of fleece,

            a knuckle thrust
back to its original joint.

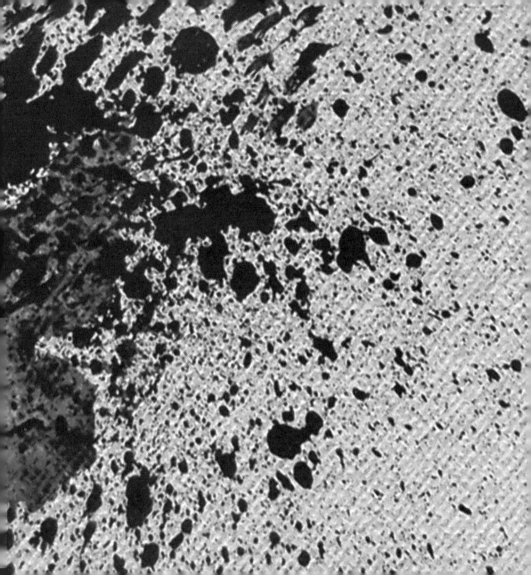

Instar (d)

We speak of how destination means little after
arrival – home a far place, an atlas of photophores
returning to tongue.

Dialect.

Warm for another night we gather sheets of
limestone to our necks, 84 days since the last
marlin breached the sea. We move with the land,
our boats held still.

Abdominal gills. Paranotal
lobes.

It's simple kinematics
we lack –

                direct flight muscles
                atrophied,

        airfoil run aground.

There are no secrets among
invertebrates,

                nymphs that consume
                the last of the light,

        the moon.

extensive

ceremony

There where
some days that
the fish would turn
into birds.
There was
no explanation.

(35.21°N 24.91°E)

Our steps curve upon themselves. Escher's infinities leave us widowed, bound to inward vectors. No longer seeking breadth, iron-flecked winds strain against our legs, tessellate and interlock. We came to the morass as wayfarers, architects trafficking in illusion. Our own faces everywhere, we hungered to build a veneer, shut ourselves behind walls resilient enough to house Achilles. In time our frames have evolved – the cold heaving quills of lead through our veins.

Spring, a sagging motel where no hill stands.
Flames expand charred wire,

    information processed

            in the olfactory,
            reflexive
limits reached.

                              to an unbound point
                    the shortest distance
             pulled free of lift,
the sky a bridge

the sky a bridge –
             an insurgent balloon
                    resisting the unaneled
                          dynamics of flight

imagine an empty   harmon

we simply do ordinary

ember this   sorrow

we are looking.

d invite what has happened

Each day we wake leaner,
listen for bells
in another village.

We've been losing roads.

Off course, I challenge
you with an untaught hold –

sputter timbre that can't
be returned to voice.

Lord, the plagues
have equalled
and equalled and equalled.

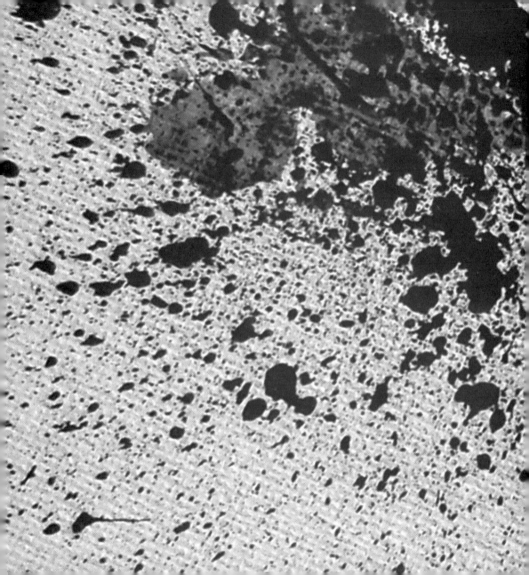

Instar (e)

Leaves drift, bibles half-open in our heads.
Expanding, light roots above the tree line, snags
the horizon. Who knew to look for time in the
slant of wings, limbs bending into shallow water?
We struggle up the roof prepared to land
anywhere – its face soft, the grit of shingles
between our toes. On its surface we learn the ache
of height, hurl a flowerpot to the ground below.
Later we recline on a coarse strip of sand – spit
testing the sky, falling.

Left wing a reconstructed fin

Left wing monogrammed
with flight coordinates

Left wing behind curfew

Left wing the distance
negotiated by a corkscrew

Right wing consoled by rainfall

Right wing a simple
intermediate

Right wing a pleated blueprint

Right wing the evolution of
papier mâché

Materials: Dissection

Adult locust, living
Specimen tube, 1
Ethanol, 70% IDA, Hazcard 40A
Stereomicroscope
Microscope, monocular up to x400 magnification
Adult locust, dead
Tray with layer of hard wax
Fine-pointed scissors, 1; pins, 8; forceps, 1; seeker, 1
Volume of insect saline or water
Watchglass, 1
Microscope slide, 2
Methylene blue, 0.5% aqueous
Coverslip, 2
Mounted needles, 2
Pipettes, 2

Optional

Impatiens, 1 fresh leaf

Intent on departure, we unclothe the trunk of an asp, set about creating wings. Thread is unspooled – feathers sewn to leaves, wax smoothed to the resistance of skin. Sweeping into the air we're inhabited by stillness, hawklike above the waves. Gesture unimportant – flight the streak of ink marking a page.

Life is
gazing back
without strings,

Descent more conjurable
than breath

       we smooth our
       feathered arms,

   taste

ballooned capillaries,
terrible unsweetened
lengths of sky.

$$(\text{L/D})_{max} = \frac{1}{2}\sqrt{\frac{\Pi A \in}{C_{D,0}}}$$

Glide ratio approaching 60:1,
I'm the first bird you've ever seen.

A cunning archetype.

As a child you imitated
prey – father dressed
as Grey Owl,

a glorious shuttlecock
dancing in aboriginal drag.

We climb beyond.

At this altitude, we learn how
little separates us
from the Pacific, its land-

bound trusses.

We've tested this before – palm thrust to glass in facsimile, skin fattened into a butterfly. Not a hand, but the language of fingers – a little heat where there were nerve fibres, dendrites. Before flight, we were certain of a window's strength. Now your fist shivers through glass, wrist locked in knots of blood, insects crowding excavation.

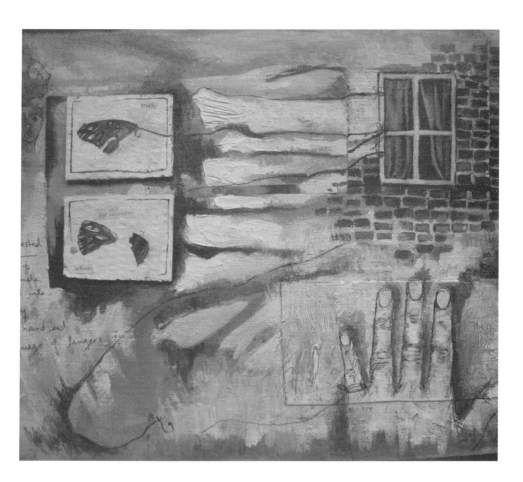

Alone again. Drunk on ribs of ash
and false light.

      Adhesive.

      Your blue shirt hangs
      from its cuffs on the line,

windblown – heat pulled free
one arm
      before the other.

Descending, you bend your digits
towards the sea in dive,

      in divination.

And there were these moments where I was pulled free

Hung from its cuffs on the line

Diminishing Lines for a Biped

It could be that
we aren't
supposed to
know this
weightlessness,
the comforts of
a quiet home.
Long before,
without flight,
all we had were
mouths of rope,
teeth and
distance. Now,
sloping
downwards, I
arrive with the
sun's
bewildered
curve and spill,
arms suspended
in the sky's
inferno.

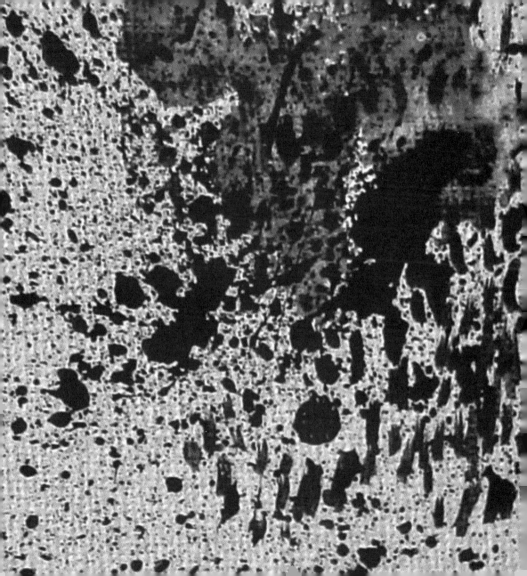

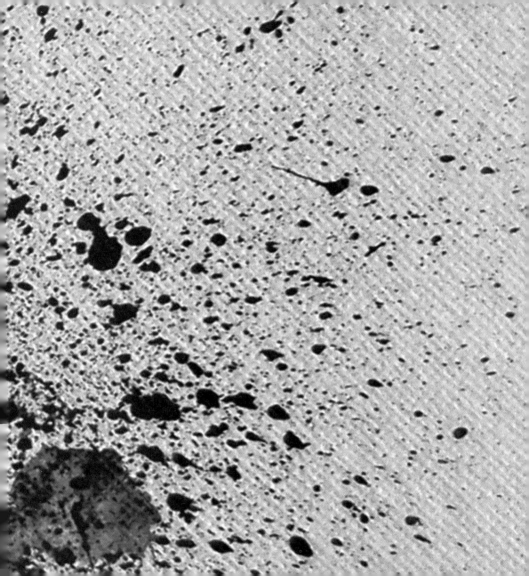

Notes

Page 11

On December 16, 1942, the HMS *Firedrake* was the escort leader of convoy ON153 with forty-three ships bound for Canada. At 20:10, the ship was hit by a torpedo fired by Uboat *U211* and broke in two. Two hours later, the HMS *Sunflower* managed to pull twenty-seven survivors from the North Atlantic Ocean.

Remerciez, Madame Forget were the last words spoken by Louis Riel before his execution on November 16, 1885.

Page 12

"I wake in the ash and the wind of the night" is adapted from pg. 1 of Cormac McCarthy's *The Road.*

Page 14

Socrates claimed that locusts were once human.

Page 15

Taxonomic classification of biblical plague locusts *(Schistocerca Gregaria)*.

Page 18

Erasure performed on text taken from Cormac McCarthy's *The Road* (pg. 2). "In any old hotel room, an old upright" – Victor Coleman, *Parking Lots.*

Page 19

Erasure performed on "Insect Biology and Recognition" found at http://ethiopia.ipm-info.org/insect_pests_ethiopia/Schistocerca_gregaria.htm

Page 21

"I see the raccoon slither into trees of our own light's making" – Victor Coleman, *Light Verse.*

Page 24

Names taken from the Book of Numbers in *The Authorized King James Version of The Holy Bible.*

Page 27

"We search for the miraculous in everything" – Victor Coleman, *Speech Sucks.*

Page 28

Conservation of mir-133 target site in the *pale* gene of locust (lmi) and12 Drosophila species. From Wei, Y., Chen, S., Yang, P., Ma, Z. and Kang, L. Characterization and comparative profiling of the small RNA transcriptomes in two phases of locust. *Genome Biology* 2009, 10:R6.

Page 31

"On the tenth day we reached the land of the Lotus-eaters, who live on a food that comes from a kind of flower… which was so delicious that those who ate of it left off caring about home, and did not even want to go back and say what had happened to them" – Homer, *The Odyssey IX*.

Whale Spectrogram, found at http://www.listenforwhales.org/NetCommunity/Page.aspx?pid=444

Page 38

"As far as the eye could reach the fields were covered by the locusts, and even the street in front of the American Consulate had the appearance, in the movement of green and black, of a flowing river." – *The New York Times*, November 21, 1915.

"…the power and glory forever and ever. Amen" from the *Lord's Prayer*.

Page 39

"sky clearing moon" – Fred Wah, *Waiting for Saskatchewan.*

Page 40

"Because these wings are no longer wings to fly / But merely vans to beat the air" – T. S. Eliot, *Ash Wednesday.*

Page 43

Source text taken from Charles Darwin's *Origin of Species.*

Page 44

"Freedom is nothing else but a chance to be better" – Albert Camus, *Resistance, Rebellion, and Death.*

Page 45

Attica is a region in Greece that contains Athens, and it is a prison facility in New York. On September 9, 1971, a prison riot resulted in the death of thirty-nine people, including ten correction officers and civilian employees. In 1975 Al Pacino starts a chant of "Attica" in the film *Dog Day Afternoon* in reference to the excessive force used by the police during the Attica riot.

Page 50

"84 days since the last marlin breached the sea" inspired by Earnest Hemingway's *Old Man and the Sea*.

Page 52

The two main theories on the origin of insect flight are that wings developed from paranotal lobes or that they are modifications of movable abdominal gills as found on the aquatic naiads of mayflies. From Grimaldi, David (2005). *Evolution of the Insects*. New York, NY: Cambridge University Press.

Page 55

Locusts are used as models in many fields of biology, especially in the field of olfactory, visual and locomotor neurophysiology.

Page 58

"I have been losing roads / and tracks and air and rivers and little thoughts…" – Dionne Brand, *Land To Light On*.

"There was always the 'untaught hold' / by which the master defeated / the pupil who challenged him." – Michael Ondaatje, *Handwriting.*

Page 65

     From http://www.practicalbiology.org/areas/advanced/cells-to-systems/ventilation-systems/dissection-of-the-ventilation-system-of-a-locust,85,EXP.html

Page 69

     L/D equation refers to the maximum lift-to-drag ratio that can be achieved during flight.

George Fetherling once described John Thompson as "a mysterious poet (who I always thought looked in photographs as Grey Owl would have looked without his aboriginal drag) who also killed himself."

Page 72

     "My blue shirt hangs from the cuffs on the line" – John Thompson, *Stilt Jack.*

Page 74

     "The comforts of a quiet home" – Victor Coleman, *Stranger.*

Acknowledgements

Fragments of *Sunday, the locusts*, often in previous incarnations, appeared in *Carousel, dANDelion, Grain, Rampike* and *The Windsor Review*.

Thanks to the editors: Kathleen Brown, Emily Carr, Karl Jirgens, Mark Laliberte and Sylvia Lergis.

An early draft of the manuscript was shortlisted for the 2009 *Matrix* Lit-Pop Award.

About the Poem

Sunday, the locusts was written by Jim Johnstone, illustrated by Julienne Lottering, arranged by Ray Hsu and designed by Karen Correia Da Silva.

Jim wishes to thank his family: Jim + Gloria Johnstone, Chris + Ashley Johnstone, Iain Johnstone, Jim + Audrey Johnstone, Frank + Helen Treml, and his partner, Erica Smith. For editorial advice and friendship, thanks to Melanie Audette, Darren Bifford, John Challis, Evie Christie, Julie Crawford, Nyla Matuk, Shane Neilson, Sandy Pool, Blair Trewartha, Halli Villegas, Myna Wallin, Shirarose Wilensky and Ian Williams.

Julie would like to thank: my mother for her spirit, sense of magic and the vivid colour that she brings into my life. Also my father, who bolstered me when he advised me to be bolder. To my brother Gavin who enlightened me about creative thinking, and my brother Graeme who inspired narrative. I would also like to thank Clare and Jim Keith who housed me when I started this project and have shown me enormous kindness. Lastly, to my husband Sean who was the constant soundtrack as I made this art and who has been Atlas during the heaviest of times.

About the Authors

Jim Johnstone holds an MSc in Reproductive Physiology from the University of Toronto, where he is currently a doctoral candidate. He is the author of two previous books of poetry: *Patternicity* (Nightwood Editions, 2010) and *The Velocity of Escape* (Guernica Editions, 2008).

Julienne Lottering was born in South Africa and is currently a Masters candidate in Art History at the University of Toronto. Her work has been exhibited in Toronto, Lyon, and New York, and has appeared on the cover of *Life and the Sheath of Enlightenment.*

Photographer: Noah Gano

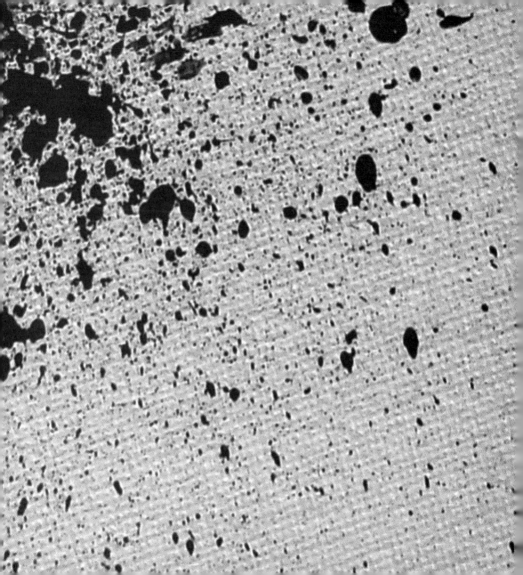

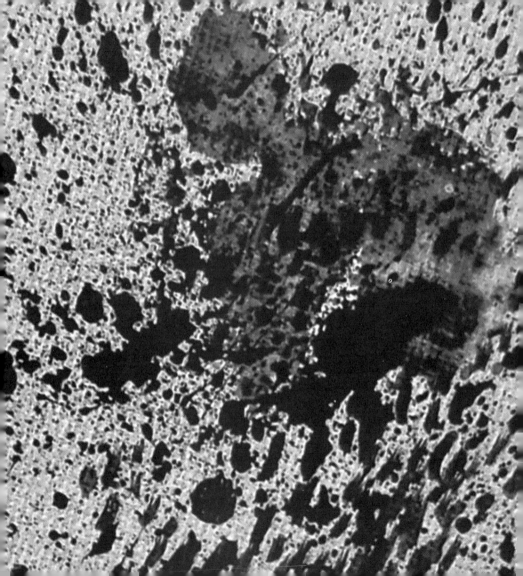